THOUGHTS ON STEWARDSHIP
Volume Two

by
Rodney M. Howard-Browne

R.M.I. Publications
Tampa, Florida

Thoughts on Stewardship, Volume Two
ISBN 1-884662-02-1
Copyright © 1995 by
Rodney M. Howard-Browne
P.O. Box 292888
Tampa, FL 33687 U.S.A.

Published by
R.M.I. Publications
P.O. Box 292888, Tampa, FL 33687 U.S.A.
P.O. Box 3900, Randburg 2125 South Africa
P.O. Box 24, Liphook, Hampshire, GU30 74X United Kingdom

CONTENTS

ACKNOWLEDGEMENT

Special thanks to my good friends Norman and Eleanor Robertson for all of their hard work in helping with the compilation of these thirteen teachings to complete Volume Two. You have been a great blessing.

INTRODUCTION

It is more blessed to give than to receive.   **Acts 20:35**

A key aspect of our revivals which have supernaturally blessed thousands of believers and impacted hundreds of local churches in the United States, South Africa, Europe, and Australia is our teaching on stewardship.

At each service, before we receive the offering, I always share practical insights from God's Word concerning the plan and purpose of God to bless His people financially. Wherever we minister, we constantly receive good reports of God's financial provision in the lives of Christians. Pastors also report that the income of their local church has increased by as much as fifty to sixty percent.

Because of this and by the request of many pastors, I felt led by God to put these Christian principles of financial stewardship into print, *Thoughts on Stewardship*, Volume One and Volume Two.

I know this book will greatly bless you and it is my prayer that every pastor will boldly teach and share these insights with his congregation and that every Christian will boldly act upon these principles and thereby walk in God's abundant blessings!

Sincerely in Christ,

Rodney M. Howard-Browne

1

BLESSINGS THAT CANNOT BE CONTAINED

Bring all the tithes (the whole tenth of your income) into the storehouse, that there may be food in My house, and prove Me now by it, says the Lord of hosts, if I will not open the windows of heaven for you and pour you out a blessing, that there shall not be room enough to receive it.

Malachi 3:10

I am a traveling missionary. You could call me an evangelist. Some evangelists say that you can send your tithe wherever you wish, but I don't believe this is true. I believe that the tithe should be given to the local church.

Some people take their tithe and think that it is theirs to split up. They do whatever they want to with it. They send two percent to the "cat and dog foundation," two percent to "Mother Hubbard's cupboard," which is a feed the poor ministry, two percent to Africa, and only God knows what they do with the other four percent.

The Bible says, **Bring all the tithes into the storehouse**. Someone may say, "Well, where is my storehouse?" The storehouse is the place where you are fed the Word of God — it is your local church. If you eat at one restaurant you can't walk out and pay the bill at the restaurant across the street. When they ask you at the door, "Where are you going?" you don't reply, "Well, it's a restaurant. You're all restaurants. You're all part of the family. Why are you so jealous?" No, you pay where you eat.

Some people think a church is a church, therefore it doesn't really matter where the tithe is given. But it does. Just as you pay your bill where you eat, you must tithe where you are fed spiritually.

When you go to church, you won't find ushers keeping your tab saying,

"That will be $15 for the forty-five minute message; someone prayed for you — $20; you were baptized — $40, etc." Before you leave, you aren't handed a bill and asked for a fifteen percent gratuity.

But when you go to a restaurant, you eat and you pay. When the waitress brings you the bill, you don't say, "Oh, no. She brought me a bill. I'll never eat here again as long as I live. These people have the audacity to ask me to pay money again. Can you believe it? I've eaten here five times this last week, and they're still bringing me a bill."

No, you don't. It's a foregone conclusion. You can eat there, but you have to pay the bill. Someone might say, "Well, the Gospel is free." Yes, the Gospel is free, but it costs money to spread it.

Planting Seeds Brings Financial Freedom

Finances are necessary for a church to grow. A pastor doesn't just plant a seed and grow a building out of the ground overnight. This is one of the reasons God says, **Bring all the tithes into the storehouse.** He goes on to say,

And I will rebuke the devourer [insects and plagues] for your sakes and he shall not destroy the fruits of your ground, neither shall your vine drop its fruit before the time in the field, says the Lord of hosts.

And all nations shall call you happy *and* blessed, for you shall be a land of delight, says the Lord of hosts.

Malachi 3:11,12

But when you look at some Christians, you can't tell that they are **a land of delight**. Rather, they are a land of fright! The Word says, **...for you shall be a land of delight.** This means that there will be rejoicing in your life.

When it comes to the area of finances, I believe that God wants His Church to be set free. People say, "Well, we've seen the excesses." Does that mean that because somebody drives a car under the influence of alcohol, we will never drive again? "Bless God, as long as I live, I will never drive another automobile. There are drunkards out there on the road and I am not going to be associated with them." No, you are going to go and drive properly. Just because there are a few dingbats that go overboard in the area of finances and into excess, doesn't mean that we are never going to seek the blessings of God.

One man had a sign on his office desk. It had a little monkey and the caption coming out of the monkey's mouth said, "I've been rich; I've been poor; rich is better." You would think that if a monkey had that much sense, human beings would wake up and say, "I'll tell you what. He's got something to think about."

Poverty Is a Curse

God wants to bless you. Do you realize that poverty is a curse? Financial pressure will rob Christians of their joy, it will break up marriages, it will cause sickness. People lie awake at night trying to figure out how they are going to pay their bills.

I believe that God will touch people's lives in this area once they learn His truths regarding giving.

The only way to bring these truths to light is by teaching God's principles concerning giving. People need to be taught how to give with the right motive and attitude rather than out of ritualistic tradition. The wrong attitude says, "Well, I guess it's time to give." No, you need to worship God with your tithes and offerings **...that there may be food in My house, and prove Me now by it....**

In my services, when I call people who need a financial miracle to come to the front, I ask them, "How many of you aren't tithing?" It is amazing to see how many put their hands up. I tell them, "If you aren't going to tithe, sit down." Why? Because if they aren't prepared to give God one-tenth, they are being disobedient to the Word of God and don't have a promise on which to stand. I'm not prepared to pray for them, because I can't pray contrary to God's Word. I have had one or two people go back to their seats, but the majority stayed because they wanted to see God bring them into victory. When they begin to tithe, they will have a breakthrough.

God's Protection Over You

Somebody said, "I've been tithing for fifty years and I've never seen the blessings of tithing." What you have not seen are the times that God has taken care of you — when accidents have been averted in your life, when angels have watched over you, your house, your children, and your loved ones.

You don't fully understand the scope of God's work. Have you ever seen one of those Pink Panther movies? Everywhere he goes, someone tries to kill him. Everybody is dying around him, but he is oblivious to it. The born-again believer, who is full of the Holy Ghost, acts in the same way. The devil is shooting at him and trying all kinds of things to harm him, but the believer just keeps going on!

I encourage you in your giving. Don't be weary in well-doing and don't do it out of tradition. Give with a cheerful heart, because the Bible says,

Let each one [give] as he has made up his own mind and purposed in his heart, not reluctantly or sorrowfully or under compulsion, for God loves (he takes pleasure in, prizes above other things, and is unwilling to abandon or do without) a cheerful (joyous) giver [whose heart is in his giving].

Thus you will be enriched in all things and in every way, so that you can be generous, and [your generosity as it is] administered by us will bring forth thanksgiving in God.

2 Corinthians 9:7,11

Always be willing to give God your best.

2

SOW ABUNDANTLY, REAP ABUNDANTLY

Let him who receives instruction in the Word [of God] share all good things with his teacher [contributing to his support].

Do not be deceived *and* deluded *and* misled; God will not allow Himself to be sneered at (scorned, disdained, or mocked by mere pretensions or professions, or by His precepts being set aside). [He inevitably deludes himself who attempts to delude God]. For whatever a man sows, that *and* that only is what he will reap.

Galatians 6:6,7

Whatever a man sows, that *and* that only is what he is going to reap. This Scripture is often preached in the context of sin, which is one interpretation. But after reading the entire passage, it is clear that Paul is also talking about all the different areas of giving. You can't plant carrots and expect pumpkins; you can't plant corn and expect bananas to grow. What you sow is what you will reap.

If you sow nothing, you will reap nothing. I once heard someone say, "When the offering bucket comes by, if you don't have anything to give, just put your hand in and pretend that you have something." Do you know what the return is on that? You will have to pretend that you received.

If a farmer goes to his field and pretends to sow, he might as well go back the next day and pretend to reap. That is about as good as it is going to get.

It is important to realize that this is also true in the area of finances. When I first began in the ministry, things were difficult for us. We began by traveling in our home country of South Africa. Once, I taught at a Bible School for six weeks and they gave me $150. Looking back, those were some of the richest times of my life. God began to teach me the principles of sowing. We learned to plant what little we had. We wouldn't be doing what we are doing today if we hadn't learned to act upon God's Word even when it looked as if everything around us was failing.

Don't Let Circumstances Stop You From Giving

Many people allow circumstances to stop them from sowing. The moment they get into a tight pinch, they back off. They say, "I can't do it. I can't give, because I'm in these circumstances." But that is when you need to give, even more. Those are the times when you need to step out on the water. You have to sow and keep planting seed in order to reap a harvest.

I often go out of my way to find something that I can sow. You can give away a tie, or a dress, or anything else the Lord leads you to give. Last year, I gave over 120 ties away. Somebody asked me, "Where did you get them from?" Well, what happens when you give away ties? You reap ties. It doesn't just have to be finances. Some of you ladies have dresses in your closet that you bought to wear four or five months from now when you slim down to a certain size. Unfortunately, five months have become two years. So your closet space is filled with things that you can't really wear. You can sow those clothes in faith and be a blessing to someone in need. There is always something that you can sow.

"Well, I don't see what this has to do with revival or how it is going to help me." Let me tell you. If God can't trust you to be a good steward of your finances, how in the world is He going to trust you with the true anointing of the Holy Ghost? If you aren't faithful with $5, $10, or $100, how is He going to entrust you with the true riches that come from heaven?

Show me a person who is a giver and I will show you someone who is blessed. Show me people who put their lives down for others, and I will show you people who are blessed. Christians should go out of their way to be a blessing.

In the past, as traveling evangelists, we would often visit churches and find that the pastor and his family had no food. Although we had nothing ourselves, my wife and I would take the last of what we had and load up the carts in the grocery store in order to fill the pastor's cupboard. Then we would buy the pastor a new suit and his wife a new dress. We would leave them thinking they had died and gone to heaven.

Sometimes they would ask, "If you do this for us, how are you going to make it?" I would tell them, "I know I'm going to make it because my Bible tells me that **the liberal soul will be made fat** (Proverbs 11:25)." If somebody had told me, "You can't afford to do what you're doing." I would look at them and say, "I can't afford not to do it. Are you trying to rob me of a blessing? Are you trying to steal from my life?"

Giving Out of Your Need

When I was one of the pastors of a church in South Africa, the Lord spoke to me one day and said, "Buy the senior pastor a new sports coat." So I went to one of the other pastors and said, "I want to buy this pastor a new sports coat and I want it to be tailor made. He can choose the fabric and we will have it made for him." He said, "This is going to cost us hundreds and hundreds of dollars." So, I asked him, "Why don't we both pay half of it. At least I would give him half the coat and the sleeve. You would give him the other half of the coat and the sleeve." He said, "Sure." I didn't really have the money at that time, but I did it anyway. The senior pastor chose the fabric and we had it made for him.

A week later, as I was standing in a meeting worshipping God, a businessman walked up to me and said, "You and I are going shopping this week." I asked, "We are? Why? Why me?" He answered, "God told me to buy you a suit." I said, "Don't buy it for me. Buy it for the senior pastor." He said, "I just bought him three last week. I'm going to buy you a suit but I'm not going to get you a piece of rubbish." He bought me a $1,200 suit.

I sowed half a jacket and got a whole suit. There is a principle involved. I am not sharing something that we don't apply in our lives daily. Even now, we constantly look for opportunities to sow through the leading of the Spirit of God — not only from our ministry, but also from our personal lives.

Always Give Your Best and God Will Bless You With His Best

We teach our children that they need to sow. Every week we give them an allowance and they know that a tithe comes off their allowance. During Christmas, when our children are blessed with new toys, we teach them to take some of their toys, those that are still nice, and plant a seed. And they have great joy in giving.

This is what must be instilled in our hearts. We need to have the same Spirit that God has; for God so loved the world that He gave Jesus.(John 3:16.) Christians must become givers and stop looking at their own circumstances — "How am I going to make it, how am I going to survive?" Let's take our eyes off ourselves, look at others, and ask, "God, how can I help them succeed? How can I help them make it? How can I be a blessing?"

When you wake up in the morning, say, "God, this day I want to be a blessing to somebody in more ways than just giving a word in season. Help me to be a blessing. Show me who I can help today. Let me be sensitive to Your Spirit."

In our ministry we have endeavored, sometimes to our detriment, to help other preachers and other ministries. Many times we end up getting hurt and people tell me, "You help too many people. You need to pull back and stop helping everybody." But those who do that become tight wads and they become closed and defensive. We can't do that. So I just think, "They aren't going to stop me from being a giver. I am going to keep giving and doing what God tells me to do because I want to obey the Word of God."

Galatians 6:7-10 provides important keys concerning the laws of giving and reaping:

...God will not allow Himself to be sneered at... For whatever a man sows, that and that only is what he will reap (verse 7). I want to keep the lines of communication open between me and God concerning the area of giving.

He who sows to his own flesh (lower nature, sensuality) will from the flesh reap decay and ruin and destruction, but he who sows to the Spirit will from the Spirit reap eternal life (verse 8).

These principles can again be placed in the context of sin. However, if you sow of your finances into the eternal things of God and into His kingdom, there is going to come an increase. When you invest in the Gospel, you are sowing to the Spirit. You are helping to spread the move of God. You are actually sowing into eternity.

Don't Stop Sowing

When Christians get to heaven, they will realize that not one thing they did for the kingdom of God has gone unnoticed. God knows everything that you do and He knows your heart. The Bible says that those things which are done secretly, God will reward openly and you will see it come to pass in your life. (Matthew 6:4.)

Keeping His promises in mind,

..let us not lose heart and grow weary and faint in acting nobly and doing right, for in due time..At the appointed season...we shall reap..if we do not loosen and relax our courage and faint (verse 9).

Don't stop giving and being a blessing. Don't pull back or you will not reap the harvest that's coming to you.

So then, as occasion and opportunity open to us, Let us do good [morally] to all people [not only being useful or profitable to them, but also doing what is for their spiritual good and advantage]. Be mindful to be a blessing, especially to those of the household of faith [those who belong to God's family with you, the believers] (verse 10).

This verse tells us to do good and be a blessing every time the opportunity arises.

Some people say that they have stopped giving because they have been hurt in the past. This is the beauty about giving and about the Word. If you sowed in faith to a ministry that abused what you sowed, God will still honor and bless you because you gave with the right heart and attitude.

You can never outgive God. And if you have never stepped into this area of increased faith and blessings, then I dare you today to jump overboard. You will taste the goodness of the Lord and be blessed beyond your expectations.

3

TAKE CARE OF GOD'S HOUSE – AND HE'LL TAKE CARE OF YOURS

Is it time for you yourselves to dwell in your paneled houses while this house [of the Lord] lies in ruins?

Now therefore thus says the Lord of hosts: Consider your ways and set your mind on what has come to you.

You have sown much, but you have reaped little; you eat, but you do not have enough; you drink, but you do not have your fill; you clothe yourselves, but no one is warm; and he who earns wages has earned them to put them in a bag with holes in it.

Haggai 1:4-6

Have you ever felt that you were earning wages to put in a bag with holes? There was a time when we were so poor, the cockroaches packed their bags and left out the door. As they walked out, we overheard them saying, "We can't hang around here. These people don't even eat." I felt so bad I almost asked them to stay! I know what it is like to earn wages and put them in a bag with holes. We didn't even have a bag. We just had the holes!

Two Houses — Your House, God's House

The Word goes on to say:

Thus says the Lord of hosts: Consider your ways (your previous and present conduct) and how you have fared.

Go up to the hill country and bring lumber and rebuild [My] house, and I will take pleasure in it and I will be glorified, says the Lord [by accepting it as done for My glory and by displaying My glory in it].

Haggai 1:7,8

God is talking about two houses — your own house and His house. Under the New Covenant the house of God is the local Church, where believers meet to be fed and encouraged by a pastor.

Put God's House First

You looked for much [harvest], and behold, it came to little; and even when you brought that home, I blew it away. Why? says the Lord of hosts. Because of My house, which lies waste while you yourselves run each man to his own house [eager to build and adorn it].

Haggai 1:9

The Lord tells us through this verse that we have our priorities wrong. We are only concerned with our own house but God is telling us to put His house first. When you do this, He will put your house first. If you take care of His house, God will take care of you. Stop trying to make only yourself comfortable. Start making sure that the needs of the church are taken care of and God will meet every one of your needs. You can never outgive Him.

The Word says these are the results of taking care of yourself before God:

22

...the heavens above you [for your sake] withhold the dew, and the earth withholds its produce.

And I have called for a drought upon the land and upon the hill country, upon the grain, the fresh wine, the oil, upon what the ground brings forth, upon men and cattle, and upon all the [wearisome] toil of [men's] hands.

Haggai 1:10,11

What is the grain? It is the Word of God. There is a famine in many churches. People are starved to hear the Word of God preached with power. The Word has been spoken, but it doesn't carry the life of God. What good is a man that gets up and speaks with great eloquence if there is no anointing to back up his words.

One demonstration of the Holy Ghost is worth a thousand words. The Apostle Paul said,

I didn't come to you with enticing words of man's wisdom, but I came to you in demonstration of the Spirit of power, that your faith should not stand the wisdom of men, but in the power of God.

1 Corinthians 2:4

The drought is not only upon the Word but upon "the fresh wine," as well. This is a type of the baptism of the Holy Ghost. No longer do people get baptized in the Spirit. No longer are there wonderful baptisms and infillings of the Holy Ghost. The drought of the oil is a drought of the anointing.

The Lord spoke to me about America. He said, "There is much preaching and teaching, but there is a famine of the demonstration of the power of the Holy Ghost." You can listen to preaching all the time. I am not negating that. Thank God for good messages. But when we have to find messages just to entertain people, and every week the titles get wilder to entice people, something is wrong. People's lives become clouded even more.

What I am talking about is the lack of demonstration of the Holy Ghost and the preaching of the Word. But that isn't the only thing that is lacking. Those who are teachers need to demonstrate what they have taught. If you can't demonstrate it, don't preach it. If it doesn't work, don't peddle it.

If you have allowed your tithes to your local church to slide, you haven't been doing what is right concerning the church's ministry. You have to remember that God has raised your local church as a lighthouse in your area. The Gospel is free, but it does cost finances to get it out. Through your giving, you can be a part of the spread of the anointing, the Lord's work will advance, and the House of God will not lack.

4

THE BLESSINGS OF THE ANOINTING

Now when Jesus came back to Bethany and was in the house of Simon the leper, A woman came up to Him with an alabaster flask of very precious perfume, and she poured it on His head as He reclined at table.

And when the disciples saw it, they were indignant, saying, For what purpose is all this waste?

For this perfume might have been sold for a large sum and the money given to the poor.

But Jesus, fully aware of this, said to them, Why do you bother the woman? She has done a noble (praiseworthy and beautiful) thing to Me.

For you always have the poor among you, but you will not always have Me.

In pouring this perfume on My body she has done something to prepare Me for My burial.

Truly I tell you, wherever this good news (the Gospel) is preached in the whole world, what this woman has done will be told also, in memory of her.

Matthew 26:6-13

The first time the Lord gave me this Scripture to read during an offering, I didn't understand why He wanted me to read it. But He told me, "Some people use manipulative tactics to get money out of God's people. But, if you take My Word and share It, My people will want to obey It." He continued, "Tell them that the woman took that which was precious to her and poured it on My head. I have taken that which money cannot buy — the anointing oil of the Holy Spirit — and I will pour it on their head. She anointed Me, but I am anointing them." Then He said, "Tell them that they can't buy the anointing, because it is free and only for those who search for me and please Me."

The Fire of God

As I was reading, we had a major move of God. It was one of the strongest anointings I have ever experienced. There were people running out of the doors laughing.

As I read, the fire of God fell. This took place during the offering teaching. I thought, "Lord, I don't even know why I'm taking the offering. Nobody's going to be able to give at all. They are laughing so hard, they can hardly see to write out Your check."

It was during this service that the power of God touched my mother. It fell on her and to this day, she isn't able to tell what happened to her. If you speak to her in private and ask, "Tell us what happened to you," the same anointing falls on her and she can't tell you. She gets drunk in the Spirit immediately.

Some people think that this story is made up. But it isn't. It's very real. You wouldn't want to be caught making something like this up because you wouldn't want to mock the Holy Ghost.

The Value of the Anointing

I want you to picture what took place the day the woman anointed Jesus. You can imagine the disciples' indignation because of what she had done. She had broken a very precious alabaster box of ointment and poured it over Jesus' head. That it was very costly was probably known by all. It is as if you took a perfume that cost $1,000 an ounce and poured it over somebody's head. A five-ounce bottle would be worth $5,000. Wouldn't you think that was a waste?

But the Bible says that if you give a prophet a glass of water in the name of a prophet, you get a prophet's reward. If you do anything to any of God's servants in that name or receive that individual as the one God has sent, then you will get the reward from that ministry. **You can't buy the anointing, but by your giving you can help spread it to other cities and even other nations.**

By giving an offering to a ministry, you are anointing that ministry with something precious to you. If you use your money to do God's work, you equip that ministry to do what they have been called to do. When you give, you are putting a portion of yourself into that ministry, because that money represents your blood, your sweat, your tears, your abilities, your time, your effort, your energy, and your life. Spirit-led giving will cause a great blessing in your life.

Meditating on God's Word

I think most Christians want to obey the Word of God. The Lord said to me, "When you teach My people concerning giving and the principles of stewardship, you are actually giving them something. You are teaching them the Word of God which will build their faith. You are instilling in their hearts certain spiritual keys that will be very effective in the days to come. What I am sharing with you is worth its weight in gold."

I know this from personal experience, because these truths have changed my life.

The Lord has instructed me to go through the Bible — from Genesis to Revelation — and underline and meditate on every Scripture that talks about giving and receiving. Therefore, I have taken entire passages and meditated on them. I have been amazed to see what the Lord has promised to give us and the revelation of His Word regarding giving.

5

GIVING CAUSES PROVISION IN THE DAY OF DROUGHT

Elijah the Tishbite, of the temporary residents of Gilead, said to Ahab, As the Lord, the God of Israel, lives, before Whom I stand, there shall not be dew or rain these years but according to My word.

And the word of the Lord came to him, saying,

Go from here and turn east and hide yourself by the brook Cherith, east of Jordan.

You shall drink of the brook, and I have commanded the ravens to feed you there.

So he did according to the word of the Lord; he went and dwelt by the brook Cherith, east of the Jordan.

And the ravens brought him bread and flesh in the morning and bread and flesh in the evening, and he drank of the brook.

After a while the brook dried up because there was no rain in the land.

1 Kings 17:1-7

The prophet of God brought the Word of the Lord concerning the famine and drought that were to come. But God had made plans to sustain Elijah by sending him to the brook Cherith, where a most unusual thing happened — a raven that would normally eat the flesh of dead animals, a selfish scavenger, brought Elijah bread and flesh in the morning and bread and flesh at night.

I can picture the raven dropping the bread and meat, but I don't know where he got it. Somebody had to be baking bread and roasting meat that the raven had access to every morning and night.

After a while, the brook dried up. There was a drought in the land and the ravens no longer came because there was no reason to come. But God had another purpose for Elijah. He told him, **Arise, go to Zarephath, which belongs to Sidon, and dwell there. Behold, I have commanded a w⬤ ow there to provide for you** (1 Kings 17:9). Notice, God did not say, "I have provided a millionaire to provide for you."

Some people think that if God is going to send somebody to provide for them, it is going to be a wealthy person who has all the resources. But I have news for you. In all of our years of ministry, it hasn't been the wealthy who have supported us. It has always been the little widow woman — the one who has just enough to make it. You will find that those who have a lot usually don't support the work of God. This is because those who have a lot of money, really don't have a lot of money. Their money has them!

Money is a wonderful servant, but a terrible master. Money can buy you a house, but it can't buy you a home. It can buy you a giant wedding, but it can't buy you a marriage.

Trust in God Even If You Are At the End of Your Rope

God didn't send Elijah to a millionaire. Instead, He said,

I have commanded a widow there to provide for you. So he arose and went to Zarephath. When he came to the gate of the city, behold, a widow was there gathering sticks. He called to her, Bring me a little water in a vessel, that I may drink.

1 Kings 17:9,10

That seemed like a reasonable request. If a man of God asked you for a glass of water, you would gladly oblige, even in times of famine. You would do your best to give him water. But Elijah went a step further. As the woman went to get the water, he called to her and said, **Bring me a morsel of bread in your hand**. In other words, he said, "I don't only want something to drink, I want something to eat."

Here is a stranger telling her to fix him something to eat. She replied,

As the Lord your God lives, I have not a loaf baked but only a handful of meal in the jar and a little oil in the bottle. See, I am gathering two sticks, that I may go in and bake it for me and my son, that we may eat it — and die.

1 Kings 17:12

This was to be her last supper. She was at the end of her tether and didn't know what to do. She was going to take the little she had and bake a meal. Then, she and her son were going to eat it and die.

Don't Let Fear Stop You From Receiving God's Blessings

Elijah said:

Fear not; go and do as you have said. But make me a little cake of [it] first and bring it to me, and afterward prepare some for yourself and your son. For thus says the Lord, the God of Israel: The jar of meal shall not waste away or the bot-

tle of oil fail until the day that the Lord sends rain on the earth.

She did as Elijah said. And she and he and her household ate for many days. And the jar of meal was not spent nor did the bottle of oil fail, according to the word which the Lord spoke through Elijah.

1 Kings 17:13-16

This woman came into an abundant supply because the oil and the meal didn't waste away. She probably opened "Zarephath Oil Company and Bakery."

What would you do if you had an abundant supply of oil and bread in a time of famine? You would call your neighbors, your friends, and your family, "Come over here. I've got enough. If you are running out of oil, come over here. I've got some and it doesn't run out. Come see what God has done."

The Word says that she and her household ate for many days. This woman took a little and God increased it. God is in the multiplication business. It is amazing how some people try to explain miracles away. One theologian got up in front of his Bible School and made this statement: "The miracles of the Bible are not such great miracles. Let's take the crossing of the Red Sea, for example. We have studied it and found that certain parts are only five inches deep, so it wasn't really a great miracle." One of his students stood up and said, "Mr. Theologian, that's even a greater miracle, because it means that God drowned the whole Egyptian army in only five inches of water!"

Every Little Bit Helps

Take the parable of the loaves and the fishes. God fed a multitude with very little. He was in the multiplication business then, as He is today. God can take a little and make it much when you put it into His hands.

It isn't the amount that you give that is important, but the attitude in which you give it. Trusting God's Word as you sow will cause the blessing of God to come into your life.

Someone said, "But I only have a little bit." I have a story about the "little bits." Mr. Little Bit and Mrs. Little Bit lived in a little bitty house at the foot of Little Bit Mountain on Little Bit Street, with the three Little Bit kids, two Little Bit dogs, and one Little Bit cat. And a man walked up to them and said, "Mr. Little Bit, how in the world do you and Mrs. Little Bit live in your little bitty house at the foot of Little Bit Mountain on Little Bit Street with three Little Bit kids, two Little Bit dogs, and one Little Bit cat? How in the world do you make it?" And he smiled and said, "It's very easy. Every little bit helps."

You might say, "Well, I only have a dollar. That's all I have." It doesn't matter. You need to start somewhere. God knows what you have and wants to bring you into His provision. God knew that the widow woman only had a little bit. In the natural, it seemed as if the prophet of God was robbing from her. But the woman needed to give the meal; she needed to give the bread more than the prophet needed to eat it. In giving it, she came into an abundant supply.

I want to encourage you to never be discouraged about your giving. Always mix faith with what you give. Worship God with your tithe. Say, "Lord, I am giving this directly to You. I thank You because You know exactly what I need. I am sowing a seed and expecting to receive."

People have told me, "We shouldn't give expecting to receive anything." That is ridiculous. When you plant a crop, you expect a harvest. Whatever you plant, whatever you sow, that is what you will reap. If you sow sparingly and grudgingly, you will reap sparingly and grudgingly, but if you sow bountifully, you will reap bountifully.

6

GOD'S DELIVERANCE BRINGS ABUNDANCE

He (talking about God) **brought [Israel] forth also with silver and gold, and there was not one feeble person among their tribes.**

The Lord spread a cloud for a covering [by day], and a fire to give light in the night.

[The Israelites] asked, and He brought quails and satisfied them with the bread of heaven.

He opened the rock, and water gushed out; it ran in the dry places like a river.

For He [earnestly] remembered His holy word and promise to Abraham His servant.

And He brought forth His people with joy, and His chosen ones with gladness *and* singing,

And gave them the lands of the nations [of Canaan], and they reaped the fruits of those peoples' labor,

That they might observe His statutes and keep His laws [hearing, receiving, loving, and obeying them]. Praise the Lord! (Hallelujah!)

Psalm 105:37,39-45

The Israelites were delivered from bondage and slavery in Egypt under the old covenant. During Passover night, prior to their deliverance, God instructed them to sacrifice a lamb, drain its blood into a bowl, and spread it on the doorposts and lintels of their houses. After doing this, they roasted the lamb and weren't allowed to leave Egypt until they had eaten it. The Passover act symbolized a type of salvation — the crossing into the place that God had prepared for them.

After leaving Egypt, the Israelites wandered for forty years in the wilderness because of their disobedience and their idolatry. The journey that should have taken just a few days took them forty years because they were a generation of fearful people who were unable to trust God. However, the Lord brought them out with silver and gold and the Bible says that there were none who were sick or feeble among them.

After most of the old generation had died, God raised strong, mighty men who would be willing to follow God's direction and boldly take the promise land. However, the spies that were sent to scout the land brought two different types of reports. One was a positive report of faith brought by Joshua and Caleb; the other was one of doubt and fear. The unbelievers said,

It is a land overflowing with milk and honey, but it is a land with giants that eat up the inhabitants. The sons of Anak dwell there. We are grasshoppers in their sight.

Numbers 13:27,33

The Israelites didn't listen to Joshua and Caleb, but decided to follow the doubters and unbelievers. In spite of that, God honored the faith of the faithful and brought them into a land of milk and honey.

Their deliverance out of Egypt represented freedom from slavery or from an environment of oppression and sin. Crossing the Red Sea represented the baptism in water. Taking the land of Canaan represented living on this earth by faith. This means that God has made abundant provisions for His children. However, the land is filled with giants that need to be defeated before we are able to enjoy the blessings.

Our God Is El Shaddai, the God Who Is More Than Enough

The Israelites had come out of the desert into the promised land, but they had giants to face. There were still cities to take. People think that the promise land is pie in the sky, that it will come sometime in the future. But the promise land under the new covenant is here, today, for the Church. Have you ever heard the hymn that says, "When we all get to heaven, what a great day of rejoicing that will be." Well, I don't think we need to wait for heaven in order to rejoice. God desires for His children to have the victory down here first.

Some say, "I can't wait to get to heaven because when I get there, I will have the armor of God." I usually ask people who make this statement, "Please tell me why would you need the armor of God in heaven? Others say, "When I cross over into the promise land, it will be wonderful to have no burden to bear. Here on earth I wander like a beggar through the heat and cold, because God leads some of us through the fire and some of us through the flood and we all end up in the mud."

Some of those old hymns are literally embalmed with unbelief. People sing hymns that weren't written by the Spirit of God, but out of a certain experience. Don't base what you believe on your experiences. Instead, believe on the Word of God.

If God delivered the Israelites under the old covenant, how much more is He going to do for us under the new covenant? The Word says that the new covenant is based upon better promises. It has been signed and sealed with the blood of the Lord Jesus Christ. Therefore, I am confident that He both desires to and is able to provide abundantly for you and me, today. Remember that God is not only the deliverer but He is also the Provider. He is Jehovah-Jireh, our Provider. He is El Shaddai, the God that is more than enough, the all-sufficient One, the God of plenty.

Don't Let Go of the Good News

You would think that the truth of redemption and abundant provision is bad news for some believers. There are some people who don't accept their deliverance, but want to live in defeat. You ask them how they're doing and they reply with, "I don't know what I'm going to do. I'll tell you, if I can make it another day, I'll be so happy. The devil did this and that. He beat me up. My dog committed suicide and the refrigerator blew up. I just don't know what to begin to do. I don't know how we can make it. If God can get me through another day, just one more day...." No wonder they don't live victoriously. No wonder they walk around looking like they were baptized in lemon juice! I am tired of long-faced believers. These are the people who sit in poverty, in sickness and disease, and don't dare to believe God for their deliverance.

The Word says that God brought forth His people with joy. When God delivers you, He *really* delivers you. Once, at church, I walked up to a lady sitting in the back and said, "Sister, have some joy." She looked up at me and snapped back, "I had the joy of the Lord a long time before you got here." I wanted to say, "Lady, your bandage has come off." I nearly called the ushers to come and embalm her again. I am not trying to pick on her, because I know that there are many people like her who are well-meaning believers.

But what they don't realize is that their salvation entitles them to soundness, wholeness, healing, preservation, deliverance, and God's blessings. The good news of the Gospel is that everything is wrapped up in salvation. It is an all-encompassing term. Some people are walking in one-quarter of their salvation. They are barely saved and God wants to fill them up and set them free.

Allowing God's Truths to Set Us Free Brings Financial Blessings

There are many blessings available to you once God's powerful truths about deliverance become a reality. This includes blessings in the area of your finances. You will rise up and realize that the devil of poverty doesn't have to be a part of your life. Jesus Christ bore the curse for you and under the new covenant, you have been redeemed. But this doesn't happen automatically. You have to stand upon the Word of God and appropriate His promises.

When you tithe, you are standing upon the Word and believing for a return. You are worshipping Him. Your money represents you, and is being invested into eternity, into the kingdom of God. When you sow, expect a harvest. I encourage you to put your faith into action and pray as follows. "God, every dollar sown represents a soul that is going to be saved. I thank You that this will come into my account. Every dollar sown will represent a church revived and a ministry set on fire." Ask God what He would have you give and follow his leading. Don't be like some who say, "I'm afraid to ask God in case He tells me to give a big amount." Imagine the type of blessing God has in store for you if you give much. You know the devil wouldn't tell you to do that because He knows that if you give generously, you will receive a generous return.

7

GIVE FREELY AND EXPECT A HARVEST OF BLESSINGS

Then the people rejoiced because these had given willingly, for with a whole *and* blameless heart they had offered freely to the Lord. King David also rejoiced greatly.

I know also, my God, that you try the heart and delight in uprightness. In the uprightness of my heart I have freely offered all of these things. And now I have seen with joy your people who are present here offer voluntarily *and* freely to You.

1 Chronicles 29:9,17

David took great pleasure in watching his people give to God willingly, although under the old covenant they had to give by law. Today, we should rejoice even more in our giving, for we have been freed from the law of sin and death and have been brought into grace. There are people who become upset when pastors talk about giving. They don't realize that when you give to the work of God, you don't give for the benefit of the ministry alone. Sure, the ministry needs to be taken care of in order to go forward. But giving is for your benefit also. If you don't give, you won't be blessed.

People who don't believe in tithing never tithe. Instead, they argue whether they should or shouldn't give. And then they say, "Well, I don't believe in tithing." That's why they aren't blessed.

I want to obey God and the least I can do is give back to Him one-tenth of what He has provided for me. I am going to go above and beyond in my tithes as well as in other areas. When your giving is directed by the Spirit of God you may give to people and ministries, who in the natural, you might not want to give to. For example, I have given to people in the past and have been told, "How dare you give that person something. You know they are going to abuse you." I always reply, "I didn't give because I thought they would abuse me or bless me. I gave because God told me to give to them. The Bible says that love covers a multitude of sins, so I am going to give to them."

Don't Let the Devil Steal Your Reward

You are in trouble if you give so that others do good things for you. People who do this are trying to buy favors. This type of giving isn't Spirit-led. In the past, God has instructed me to give to ministers who have criticized our ministry and run us down. The first time the Lord asked me to do this, I said, "No, I'm not going to do that. I'm not. Did you hear what they said? They stood up in church and said this and that about me. The only thing I am going to do is give them a piece of my mind." And the Lord said, "Don't you do that. The last time you did that, you nearly gave away all the mind you had!"

Some people only want to help those who are in a position of power. They would never help someone who can't offer them anything. From time to time, we meet people who are millionaires. The first thing I say is, "I don't want one dime of your money. Keep it. If I can help you in any way, I will. You aren't going to buy into my ministry and you aren't going to dictate to me."

I have helped people who have been abused and battered. Their names have been slandered and people have told me, "Don't get involved with that person and help them. Your name will be dragged through the mud." But I tell them, "I don't have a name." Jesus ate at the tax collector's house. He ate with the publicans and sinners. If you can't reach down to people who are lower than you are, you need to lose your name, because it isn't worth much.

God has told me on many occasions that He would bring to us ministers who had been bruised, battered, and who had gone through destructive things in their lives. He also said, "Don't turn any one of them away. I am going to restore ministers who have fallen. Many of them have come through fire but My anointing will rest upon them again for I am the God Who restores." Then He reminded me of Samson and said, "Be very careful how you treat My servants."

But the Greatest of These Is Love

God will not forget your labor of love. Ask yourself, "How would Jesus react if He came to your house today? Would He remember your past or would He look at you and love you?

Peter, who walked with Jesus, denied Him three times. After Jesus was resurrected, He was on the beach and Peter came on shore. Jesus looked at him. He didn't say, "Peter, I will never trust you again. It will take at least a year to build My confidence back in you. You stabbed Me in the back. You let Me down in My darkest hour. Peter, I knew I could never trust you. I always knew that you would let Me down." He never said any of those things. Instead, He looked at Peter and asked, "Peter, do you love Me?" Don't you think that cut more than anything? Don't you think it was like a sharp sword going right in. And Peter said, "Lord, You know I love You." "Peter, do you love Me? Then feed My sheep."

If Jesus came to your house today, He wouldn't remember your past or bring any allegations against you. He would look at you with His loving eyes and say, "I love you." And He would put His arms around you and pull you to Himself.

When the religious leaders were brought to the woman who was caught in adultery, they carried stones and were ready to kill her. Jesus bent down and wrote in the sand with His finger. I wonder what He wrote. I think I have some idea. Let's say the first man's name was Abe. Jesus wrote, "Who was that woman you were with last night, Abe?" And old Abe dropped his rock and walked away. When He had finished writing the revelations in the sand — which we will never know until that day when we stand face to face before Him — every rock was on the ground and every man had walked away. **Let him who is without sin among you be the first to throw a stone at her** (John 8:7b). Let's remember that love — for God and then for our neighbor — is God's primary command-ment given to us under the New Covenant.

The last thing that Jesus did before He left the earth was to wash the disciples' feet. When you stand before Him on judgement day, it isn't how sanctimonious and self-righteous you have been that counts. It will not be whether you did this or that, but whether you loved your brothers and sisters and reached out to them with compassion and mercy.

The Church has to become more loving, more forgiving, and more giving. It begins with a commitment to your local church, the place where you are fed the Word of God. I believe that God looks at people's hearts and motives when it concerns their giving. You can throw thousands of dollars in the offering bucket with the wrong motive but that is like planting dead seeds. You will never reap from that offering. But you can give $5 with a pure and loving heart and see the blessings of God come into your life.

If you haven't been tithing, get with the program — give

your tithe to your church. I believe God expects that from you. If you can't do this, don't come to the prayer line and expect to be blessed, because in God's eyes obedience is better than sacrifice. Make a decision to tithe and give freely. Then, get ready to experience God's goodness in Your life.

8

GIVING OUT OF YOUR NEED WILL BRING A BREAKTHROUGH

And He (Jesus) **sat down opposite the treasury and saw how the crowd was casting money into the treasury. Many rich [people] were throwing in large sums...Truly *and* surely I tell you, this widow, [she who is] poverty-stricken, has put in more than all those contributing to the treasury.**

Mark 12:41,43b

In the days of Jesus there were no checks with which to pay the tithe, so people would bring their bags of money to the treasury. The wealthy would take longer in their giving. Everyone would know how much each person gave. Let's say it took two or three minutes to get one guy out of the way. Maybe he was the head of a large corporation — Abraham and Sons. It would take him longer to give his money than it would someone coming with a little bit. People could actually watch how much time people took over their giving. Jesus was doing just that. He was watching what each person gave. How would you feel if Jesus Christ Himself was standing in front of you as you gave your offering? You would probably come with a different attitude, wouldn't you?

The Scripture goes on to say,

And a widow who was poverty-stricken came and put in two copper mites [the smallest of coins], which together make half of a cent.

Mark 12:42

She didn't put in $100 or $500 or $1,000 or $5,000. She put in half of a cent — a half-penny. But Jesus saw it. It probably didn't go clang-clang-clang against the other coins. It probably just went tinkle-tinkle.

And He called His disciples [to Him] and said to them, Truly *and* surely I tell you, this widow, [she who is] poverty-stricken, has put in more than all those contributing to the treasury.

For they all threw in out of their abundance; but she, out of her deep poverty, has put in everything that she had — [even] all she had on which to live.

Mark 12:43,44

Jesus said, "She has put in more than the others have put in." In the natural, the widow woman had probably given the smallest amount. But God isn't looking at the amount that you give, He looks at your heart. It is the attitude in which you give that has a direct correlation to what you receive.

Mix Faith With Your Giving

If you don't mix faith with your giving, God won't accept your money. God wants you because when He has you, He has your money as well. He has everything that you are. As believers, it is important that we see this. I don't believe we can discriminate between someone who gives a large amount and someone else who can only put a quarter or a dollar into the offering. The issue isn't how much a person gives. There are people who could give $10,000 and not miss it because God has blessed them with an abundance. Those people rejoice and give out of their overflow. But the widow woman wasn't giving out of her savings or her nest egg. She was giving out of her need. She gave out of her deep poverty, out of what she had to live on. That was all the money she had to buy food and pay her rent. In today's terms, that money was what she would have used to pay the gas company.

God Looks at the Heart

God isn't concerned with the outward appearance. When we bring our gifts to Him, He looks at the heart of the individual. You should rejoice about this. Many times, people who have gone through trials in their finances think, "I'm not worthy because I bring this little offering." I want you to understand that it isn't in the amount, it is in the attitude of faith; it is only by mixing faith with giving, that you will see the blessings of God break through in your life.

It doesn't matter if you only have a little bit to give. Some people think, "If I put $5 in the offering, how will that help the church? It's only $5." What they don't see is that you aren't giving because the church needs the money, you are giving because you need to honor God with your substance. You have to take the focus off the needs of the church and off your personal needs. What should your focus be? You should focus on being a good steward of the finances God has entrusted to you.

Honor the Lord with your capital *and* sufficiency [from righteous labors] and with the firstfruits of all your income;

So shall your storage places be filled with plenty, and your vats shall be overflowing with new wine.

Proverbs 3:9,10

9

PUT YOUR TRUST IN GOD

Thus says the Lord: Cursed [with great evil] is the strong man who trusts in and relies on frail man, making weak [human] flesh his arm, and whose mind and heart turn aside from the Lord.

For he shall be like a shrub or a person naked and destitute in the desert; and he shall not see any good come, but shall dwell in the parched places in the wilderness, in an uninhabited salt land.

[Most] blessed is the man who believes in, trusts in, and relies on the Lord, and whose hope and confidence the Lord is.

For he shall be like a tree planted by the waters that spreads out its roots by the river; but its leaf shall be green. It shall not be anxious and full of care in the year of drought, nor shall it cease yielding fruit.

Jeremiah 17:5-8

God doesn't want your mind and heart on anything else but Him. He wants you to trust Him. If Christians don't learn how to trust God while things are good — and believe me, they are good — I don't know how they will make it to the end of the nineties, if Jesus tarries. I believe that things aren't going to get better, because we are living in the closing of the ages.

Evil men and seducers are going to wax worse. In the Church, there is going to be mighty revival, but in the world, terrible turmoil. Only those who know how to believe God and walk by faith are going to make it in these last days. Some Christians are going to literally tear their hair out; hearts are going to fail them for fear because they haven't learned to trust God. They have always looked to someone else to help them make it. If you aren't a giver, you won't make it.

True Shepherds Care for the Flock of God

As ministers of the Gospel, as shepherds of the flock of God, we are responsible to shear the flock, not to fleece it. There is a difference. Let me give you an example.

If you get a lamb while he is little, the family gets attached to it, feeds it from a bottle and wouldn't even think of killing or hurting it. But, a farmer who loves his sheep has a duty to sheer them when they become laden with wool. A friend of mine shared a story with me about this.

He stopped by the farm of a man who had a lot of sheep. When he looked at the sheep, they were so heavily laden with wool that disease was setting in. So my friend asked the farmer, "What are you doing?" The farmer replied, "I don't like to shear them because I might nick a little bit and don't want to hurt them. We just love them. They have been around the house since they were little."

So my friend said, "You are doing more harm by not shearing them. Those sheep don't feel the nicks. When you take the shears and begin to take the wool off of them, they will produce more wool. It is actually beneficial to them."

Sometimes there are things that we don't want to do, because of misguided thinking. People say, "If I take an offering, it will hurt people." No, you can't hurt people by taking an offering. You hurt them by giving emotional pleas for finances rather than teaching them the Word concerning giving. If they aren't giving in faith, they are being hurt. But if they are giving in faith, there is no way that they will be hurt because they are honoring the Word of God. When you honor His Word, God will honor you and bring you into a higher realm of His goodness.

Profit Not Poverty

America is the most blessed country on the face of the earth. For people to be poor in this country is often nothing more than laziness. When I go to the Bronx in New York, I tell them, "If you are living off the government, you better get off your blessed assurance and work." Someone told me that there is a shortage of jobs. But this isn't true. When an industry decreases certain jobs, employment in other areas increases. For example, the record industry was replaced by the CD industry and people could get jobs if they were willing to increase their knowledge. There are many prosperous people, even millionaires, who started out poor, but who worked very hard to get what they have.

For a child of God to live in poverty is a shame. With Jesus and the Holy Spirit on your side, you can be lead and blessed. He will show you how to profit. If anybody is going to be successful, why shouldn't it be you?

I have been young and now am old, yet have I not seen the [uncompromisingly] righteous forsaken or their seed begging bread.

Psalm 37:25

God has no room for lazy people. With His power, you can

53

rise above any circumstance and achieve greatness. There is no excuse for walking in a lack situation, especially when you have the power of God at your disposal. The Bible says.

You will show me the path of life, in Your presence is fullness of joy, at Your right hand there are pleasures forevermore.

Psalm 16:11

In His presence there is no lack, and whenever you get into the presence of God, He will show you how to profit.

Wisdom and Integrity in Finances

The Bible says that the children of the world are wiser in the affairs of finances than the children of light. These things ought not be. You have God living inside of you and He doesn't sit around waiting for someone else to do something. There are a lot of Christians who want to work in an underhanded manner. They don't pay their taxes or tithe, but still expect to receive God's blessings. They tell you tithing falls under the old covenant. This is their excuse. They aren't walking in wisdom or integrity!

If you live in America, you are blessed. Don't let the newspaper or television tell you that the economy is bad. Don't let the devil trick you into not giving and rob you of the blessing God has for you. Put your trust in God and His Word! Make God your source for He will never fail you.

10

ABRAHAM'S BLESSINGS ARE YOURS

Christ purchased our freedom [redeeming us] from the curse (doom) of the Law [and its condemnation] by [Himself] becoming a curse for us, for it is written [in the Scriptures], Cursed is everyone who hangs on a tree (is crucified);

To the end that through [their receiving] Christ Jesus, the blessing [promised] to Abraham might come upon the Gentiles, so that we through faith might [all] receive [the realization of] the promise of the [Holy] Spirit.

Galatians 3:13,14

When Jesus Christ died on the cross, He redeemed us from the curse of the law — poverty, sickness and spiritual death. For spiritual death, Jesus gave us eternal life, for sickness, divine healing and health, and for poverty, wealth.

The devil has darkened some people's minds with religious traditions and ways of thinking. He has convinced them that poverty is a virtue and a blessing. But the Bible tells us that poverty is a curse, along with sickness and sin. As Christians, we should flee poverty in the same way we flee sickness, disease, or sin.

Think the Thoughts of God

If Satan tempts you with thoughts that are against the Word of God, you should immediately find the Scripture that counteracts that thought. Then, meditate on it. Ungodly thoughts may enter your mind but you don't have to dwell on them. Remember the old saying, "You can't stop the birds from flying over your head, but you can stop them from making a nest in your hair." It isn't a sin to think an ungodly thought, but it is a sin to dwell on it.

In the same way that you would reject sin, you should reject the temptation to sin, to get sick or to live in poverty. In the winter time, everybody plans for the flu. It is advertised on television, "There is a new strain of the flu going around" and everyone gets ready to catch it. They say, "I will be the first one to get it! I am always the first one in my family to get the flu. I am expecting the flu any day now." Then suddenly they have it and say, "I told you. I am a prophet. I knew I would get sick."

These are the people who walk around expecting sickness and disease. Those thoughts come from hell not from heaven. Health and healing come from heaven. In God's presence there is divine healing. In His presence there is provision — miraculous, supernatural, abundant provision. When God walks in, sickness, disease, oppression, fear, and poverty go out the back door, because He is absolute life. We are commanded by the Word to meditate on good things and on the goodness of God.

Finally, brethren, whatsoever things are true, whatsoever things are honest, whatsoever things are just, whatsoever things are pure, whatsoever things are lovely, whatsoever things are of good report; if there be any virtue, and if there be any praise, think on these things.

Philippians 4:8 KJV

The Spirit of Poverty

Poverty can manifest itself in many ways. I know of several millionaires who are bound by a spirit of poverty. They have a poverty mentality. Although it has driven them to achieve great things in the business world, they stay awake at night worrying about how they will keep what they have achieved. The driving force in their life is a spirit of poverty. These kinds of people don't know that they are bound by this spirit. They always walk around saying, "I can't afford this. I can't afford that." If you allow it, this mentality will come and live in your house. It will affect your wife and your children who will also grow up saying, "I can't afford this. I can't afford that." They will always be penny pinching and trying to make ends meet. Don't allow this curse to take control of your family.

There are some people who think that God wants them to own things that are run down and old. One evangelist tells the story of a pastor that he met in a parking lot. The pastor was driving an old Ford — the tires were bad, the seats were falling apart, and the springs were coming through the seats. The knobs on the steering wheel were worn off. When he started his car, it backfired and belched black smoke.

The evangelist said to the preacher, "Is this your car?" and the preacher stuck out his chest and said, "Yes, this is my car." Of course, he was having problems. The car wouldn't start. He continued, "God wants me to have this car." Just as this pastor did, many people think that this mentality is one of humbleness, when in reality they are allowing the devil to stop God's blessings from coming to them.

I call this behavior "ignorance gone to seed." You are wrong if you think you are being humble by being that way. God isn't poor. And for those people who are always saying, "But what about those who have gone into excess?" Well, you can go into excess on either side — excess of poverty or of wealth. Why don't you just take the middle of the road and allow the Holy

Spirit to direct you. If your heart and motives are right, God will bless you beyond measure.

Jesus Didn't Live in Poverty

Some people think that Jesus was poor. 2 Corinthians 8:9b says, **...though He was [so very] rich, yet for your sakes He became [so very] poor, in order that by His poverty you might become enriched (abundantly supplied)**. The word *rich*, in the Greek, means to be well taken care of in the affairs of life. Jesus did become poor. It is poverty to leave the throne of glory and come down to be born in a manger. It was poverty when compared to the place from which he came. *Yet He wasn't poor.*

The gifts of gold, frankincense, and myrrh were gifts that kings would send to other kings. They were enough to make anybody a very wealthy person. We don't know what was done with His gifts, but I am sure that they funded Jesus and His parents.

God has made provisions for the family so that parents are able to properly care for their children. God wants a husband to maintain his marriage and look after his wife. Husbands, the most spiritual thing you can do for your marriage is to spend some money on your wife.

There are people who go into excess and are ruined. The Bible says that prosperity ruins a fool. But if your heart and motives are right, if you seek first the kingdom of God and His righteousness, all those other things will be added unto you. Poverty is a curse and you need to resist it from your life. Jesus has redeemed you from the curse and wants to bless you so that you may be in a position to bless others.

Make the following prayer to God your own. "Lord, make me a blessing. Let my life be a channel through which your blessings can continually flow to those who are hurting spiritually, mentally, physically, financially, and socially. Make me a blessing that I may be like Jesus."

Take Authority Over Your Finances

When Jesus went to a wedding in Canaan, there was a shortage of wine. He met the need at that moment and turned the water into wine. When people were hungry, He fed them. When they needed tax money, He took them fishing. Provision was brought about through the anointing of God.

But some people aren't blessed because they are unwise in the way they handle their money. They buy things they don't need, with money they don't even have, in order to please people they don't even like.

If your outgo exceeds your income, then your upkeep is going to be your downfall. If you are battling financially, you must put yourself on a budget and learn to stick to it no matter what. If you don't, then forget about overcoming. God can't bless an idiot! Are you tithing to your local church? God can't bless a thief. There are certain basic things which will ensure that you get on the path to financial recovery

When we were in trouble with our finances, I used to bind the devil. I would say, "Devil, I take authority over you." Every day, I would say, "I bind you and curse you from my finances." One day, as I was walking by the mirror, God said, "Do you know why the devil is attacking your finances?" I said, "Please Lord, show me. Reveal the devil that is attacking my finances." I looked in the mirror and He said, "You have just found him. The way you handle your finances, you don't need the devil to attack them. You have done a good job of attacking them yourself."

If you are doing as I did, you need to remember that it isn't the devil who is attacking your finances, but the lack of wisdom in your life. You are the one who is spending your money.

You are the one who is buying things and hoping that God will meet a need that you are creating. But if you are wise and allow the Spirit of God to lead you, He will show you what to do. He will give you insight on how to come out of the wrong approach to spending and will also direct you so that you can benefit from wise deals.

If you have a problem with overspending or overbuying, you need to take authority over that spirit. Resist it in Jesus' name. Take authority over yourself. Focus on God's Word and you will see the victory in your life.

God's blessings are available for you when your life has been dedicated to God. Don't let the spirit of poverty and its many manifestations keep the blessings of His covenant from you.

11

IF YOU DON'T USE IT, YOU'LL LOSE IT

For whoever has [spiritual knowledge], to him will more be given and he will be furnished richly so that he will have abundance; but from him who has not, even what he has will be taken away.

Matthew 13:12

Jesus spoke to the multitudes during His ministry on earth through the use of parables. One of the best-known parables is the Parable of the Talents, where we are taught about stewardship of the gifts that God has given to His children. When it talks about talents, I believe the Scripture is talking about money.

For the kingdom of God is as a man travelling into a far country, who called his own servants, and delivered unto them his goods.

And unto one he gave five talents, to another two, and to another one; to every man according to his several ability; and straightway took his journey.

Then he that had received the five talents went and traded with the same, and made them other five talents.

And likewise he that had received two, he also gained other two.

But he that had received one went and digged in the earth, and hid his lord's money.

After a long time the lord of those servants cometh, and reckoneth with them.

And so he that had received five talents came and brought other five talents, saying, Lord, thou deliverest unto me five talents; behold, I have gained beside them five talents more.

His lord said unto him, Well done, thou good and faithful servant: thou hast been faithful over many things: enter thou into the joy of thy lord.

He also that had received two talents came and said, Lord, thou deliverest unto me two talents: behold, I have gained two other talents beside them.

His lord said unto him, Well done, good and faithful servant; thou has been faithful over a few things, I will make thee ruler over many things: enter thou into the joy of thy lord.

Then he which had received the one talent came and said, Lord, I knew thee that thou art a hard man, reaping where thou hast not sown, and gathering where thou hast not strayed.

And I was afraid, and went and hid thy talent in the earth: lo, there thou has that is thine.

His lord answered and said unto him, Thou wicked and slothful servant, thou knewest that I reap where I sowed not, and gather where I have not strayed:

Thou oughtest therefore to have put my money to the exchangers, and then at my coming I should have received mine own with usury.

Take therefore the talent from him, and give it unto him which hath the ten talents.

For unto every one that hath shall be given, and he shall have abundance, but from him that hath not shall be taken away even that which he hath.

Matthew 25:14-29

At first glance it seems as if it is unfair that the person who had only one talent lost it, and the one who had more got richer. Have you ever heard the saying, "The rich get richer and the poor got poorer?" However, if you study and meditate on the Scriptures above, you will find that the Parable of the Talents, as this passage is known, contains some spiritual truths that will revolutionize your thinking in the area of giving and prospering. When you put the talents that God has given you to work for His kingdom, He will bring prosperity to your soul and to your finances.

People get upset because they only have one talent. They need to remember that it was up to the steward of the talent to make it grow. Jesus taught us that God will increase the talents of those who are faithful — especially if it means faithful with little. But the talents of those who bury them and hide them away will be given to those who are faithful.

If God can't trust you with money, He sure can't trust you with the anointing, because the money of the world is in reality the "anointing" of the flesh. If you can say of someone, "They can do anything they want to do. They are enabled and equipped to do whatever they need to," you could say they are anointed in the flesh.

Men whom God can't trust with the anointing, end up blowing themselves and their ministries out of the water. Those whose primary focus is on material things, instead of the things of God, get eaten up with worms, as Herod did in the Book of Acts.

God's Anointing Is Not For Sale

Recently I heard a story that really disturbed me. A multi-millionaire moved into a city, built a church building that seated over a thousand people, and paid for it with cash. Since there were no people in this church, he booked some well-known speakers and advertised in the local newspaper. Although this man wasn't interested in building the Body of Christ, but only in promoting an enterprise, he was able to bring speakers who weren't led by the Spirit of God. They were only interested in a first-class plane ticket, a suite in an expensive hotel, and a guaranteed honorarium of $5,000 or $10,000.

The sad thing is that the church started filling up. The man who started the church isn't even a pastor. He is a promoter and no different from a worldly entertainment broker. Every week there is a new flight staged — a renowned singer or a top preacher. This is how he is "building" the church. Attendance is nearly a thousand people. The word is that his goal is to sell it when attendance reaches its maximum. I am amazed at the means people will use to get a crowd.

Simon the Sorcerer wanted to take his money and buy the anointing. The businessman in this story bought the church and is now planning to sell it. That's prostituting the anointing of God. The sheep who attend a place like that don't know any better. They think, "We've got a growing church. We've got all these speakers coming in. My, we get fed here." They don't know they are being abused — left, right and center.

You Shall Know Them By Their Fruits

When we minister in different churches, I tell pastors all the time, "We guarantee a revival. If we don't have revival, you can have all the offerings back."

Someone said, "You guarantee revival?" Yes! I can be certain that revival will take place, because I only minister in the places where God directs me. The anointing to do God's work comes from Him. You can only minister with the anointing if you are obeying God.

There are some people who want to buy the anointing and there are ministries that allow people with money to influence them. Some people, because they are lukewarm, give the pastor a gift with strings attached to it, and say, "If you'll preach this and preach that, then we'll be favorable towards you. If you don't preach what we want, it won't be well with you." That's when I would tell them to hit the road.

You can't buy the anointing. The Bible tells us, that if God can't trust us with unrighteous mammon (money), He won't trust us with the true riches that come from heaven. If He can't trust you with $100 flowing through you, how can He trust you with His miracle-working power?

Why don't we see the miracles we saw in Jesus' days? Because most Christians aren't ready to receive the anointing. What would happen if God dropped in you the anointing for the miraculous, where incurable diseases were instantaneously healed? Could you live under that? Could your marriage stand the pressure? Does your marriage have a solid foundation? What would happen when people found out where you lived and lined up outside your house? What would you do if you were in the bath tub and a hand came through the window asking for prayer?

What do you think? Do you know what Jesus did? He healed the man and said, "Don't tell anybody about this. Receive your sight and mention none of this. Be made whole. Tell no one." Of course, he didn't. How could you?

Signs and miracles will follow those who minister God's

Word for the sake of the kingdom. This only happens when the anointing of God is on you. Being a good steward of your spiritual and financial talents will allow you to fulfill your calling on this earth, with God's abundant provision.

12

PUT GOD AND HIS WORD IN FIRST PLACE

Blessed (happy, fortunate, prosperous, and enviable) is the man who walks and lives not in the counsel of the ungodly [following their advice, their plans and purposes], nor stands [submissive and inactive] in the path where sinners walk, nor sits down [to relax and rest] where the scornful [and the mockers] gather.

Psalm 1:1

I want you to notice the progression in this Scripture. The *King James Version* says, **Blessed is the man who does not walk in the counsel of the ungodly, nor stands in the way of sinners, nor sits in the seat of mockers.** If you walk in the counsel of the ungodly, you will end up standing in the way of sinners and sitting in the seat of mockers.

People who take their eyes off the Word of God and run to some psychiatrist to get insight into the things of the Spirit will get themselves into trouble. You can't mix the things of the Spirit with the things of the world. If you follow the things of the world, you can't be blessed.

God's Word needs to take first place in your life. It should be the final authority over every circumstance. By habitually pondering and studying the things of God, you will be blessed.

But his delight *and* desire are in the law of the Lord, and on His law (the precepts, the instructions, the teachings of God) he habitually meditates (ponders and studies) by day and by night.

Psalm 1:2

God Can't Anoint a Lie

The church is trying to compete with the world. You can't do this and expect to receive a blessing. It is time for Christians to wake up and find out what they are supposed to be doing here. They are supposed to be ministering by the Spirit, not by the flesh.

For example, the Church tries to compete with the world in the area of television. Television is dangerous because it can paint a false picture. Once I went on a talk show. There was nobody in the studio but the announcer said, "We're so glad to have with us Evangelist Rodney Howard-Browne," I heard thousands of people clapping. I looked around and thought, "They must have slipped in when I wasn't looking."

The people weren't live, it was just a machine. I thought, "We don't need to have a church. Let's get a couple of machines, and do the service out of our garage. We will splice in crowd shots from some other place." Do you know that some ministries are doing exactly that? They go to one place and if they have bad crowds, they splice in crowd scenes from other crusades.

Ministries become deceitful and then wonder why the anointing of God doesn't rest on them. God can't anoint a lie. He will only anoint the truth. You can only be blessed when you walk in His Word. You can't be blessed if you walk in deceit.

Blessings Come Only Through Obedience

We preach the Word of God because we want to see revival in America. God never did tell me to find a need. He told me to do what He had called me to do. God didn't call me to save the world. Jesus will do that.

The Church is walking in the counsel of the ungodly when it comes to moving in the Spirit. That is why it isn't blessed. The Word says the following about he who delights in the law of the Lord:

And he shall be like a tree firmly planted [and tended] by the streams of water, ready to bring forth its fruit in its season; its leaf also shall not fade *or* wither; and everything he does shall prosper [and come to maturity].

Not so the wicked [those disobedient and living without God are not so]. But they are like the chaff [worthless, dead, without substance] which the wind drives away.

Therefore the wicked [those disobedient and living without God] shall not stand [justified] in the judgment, nor sinners in the congregation of the righteous [those who are upright and in right standing with God].

For the Lord knows *and* is fully acquainted with the way of the righteous, but the way of the ungodly [those living outside God's will] shall perish (end in ruin and come to nought).

Psalm 1:3-6

The people in the world are hungry for the move of God. Revival is spreading. God said, "If you disobey Me, you will be in big trouble. If you obey Me, you will be blessed." I won't do anything until I know God has told me to do it. Only do what God tells you to do. If you obey Him, you will be blessed. If you disobey Him, you will walk with the ungodly. The Word says that the ungodly, those living outside of God's will, shall perish, end in ruin, and come to naught.

I want to see the Church walking in the power of God as never before. I want to see Christians moving in a new dimension of the supernatural. I want to see another great awakening come to America. Keeping our eyes on God and walking in obedience to His Word and His ways are necessary ingredients to seeing this take place.

13

LIVING IN THE SECRET PLACE OF THE MOST HIGH

He who dwells in the secret place of the Most High shall remain stable *and* fixed under the shadow of the Almighty [Whose power no foe can withstand].

Psalm 91:1

As Christians, we should be trying to find our place in God, the secret place under the anointing of the Holy Ghost. There is a reality to the power in this verse. As God's power and anointing comes upon you, you will enter into a deeper realm of the supernatural and start living in that secret place.

The concept of living in the secret place can't be explained in the natural. It can't be understood in the natural. Enoch walked with God and was not, for God took him. He came so close to heaven that he lived in that realm of the glory.

Obviously, we still have to function in our daily lives on this earth. People are married and have children to raise. They have to be husbands or wives and work jobs in order to provide for their family. But there has to be a balance, although there is nothing to stop anybody from going as deep as they want to go in the things of God.

God can become more real to you than anybody else you know. This principle doesn't work for the Sunday morning Christian or for the carnal Christian because it doesn't work for those who are walking after the flesh.

Some people think God left them in authority to be watch-dogs of the Church and to correct it and cause it to operate the way they think it should. In the book of Acts, Gamaliel, the Pharisee, stood and said, "Leave them alone. If it is of God, it will succeed. If it isn't of God, it will come to nothing." You would think if a Pharisee had enough brains, modern-day people would have enough brains to read the Bible and find out what they need to do. Don't let other people's opinions keep you from a closer walk with God.

You have to determine to live in the secret place. Somebody once said, "Aren't you worried about the devil?" No, because when you are in the secret place, there is nothing to worry about.

Trust God's Power

I will say of the Lord, He is my Refuge and my Fortress, my God; on Him I lean *and* rely, *and* in Him I [confidently] trust!

Psalm 91:2

The Holy Spirit knows exactly where to touch people's lives. As individual Christians, it is impossible for us to reach every person in this world and meet their needs. But the Holy Spirit can. Trust that God will reveal Himself to His people. Once you taste the glory of God, you won't want anything else.

Verse 3 continues, **For [then] He will deliver you from the snare of the fowler and from the deadly pestilence**. With each of God's promises, there comes a condition. Psalm 91 doesn't just work for every believer. You have to live it in order for it to work. There are a lot of Christians who are being wiped out because they never walked in the light of Psalm 91. In these last days, this Psalm needs to become a living reality in your life because things aren't going to get better.

Don't Live in Fear

[Then] He will cover you with His pinions, and under His wings shall you trust and find refuge; His truth and His faithfulness are a shield and a buckler.

You shall not be afraid of the terror of the night, nor of the arrow (the evil plots and slanders of the wicked) that flies by day.

Psalm 91:4,5

There are people who live in fear. I know ministers who won't eat at a restaurant because they are scared that someone in the kitchen, who is a homosexual, has AIDS. They are afraid they will get AIDS from eating the food.

Or how about those people who go on health kicks because they are terrified of dying from disease. They eat bamboo shoots and roots and work out for hours each day. Then one day, as they walk across a street, a truck hits them.

There are Christians living in fear who are afraid of going out in the dark. The Word says that you won't be afraid of the terror of the night. When you are dwelling in the secret place it, fear can't get to you

God Will Protect You

Nor of the pestilence that stalks in darkness, nor of the destruction and sudden death that surprise and lay waste at noonday.

A thousand may fall at your side, and ten thousand at

your right hand, but it shall not come near you.

Only a spectator shall you be [yourself inaccessible in the secret place of the Most High] as you witness the reward of the wicked.

Psalm 91:6-8

If you are a part of the purpose and will of God, you are untouchable to the enemy. The devil can't touch you. He has no legal right to touch you. He has to move out of the way when you walk through. You can be in the middle of Baghdad and be safe in the will of God.

Because you have made the Lord your refuge, the Most High your dwelling place,

There shall no evil befall you, nor any plague *or* calamity come near your tent.

For He will give His angels [especial] charge over you to accompany *and* defend *and* preserve you in all your ways [of obedience and service].

Psalm 91:9-11

You have to make Him your refuge and your dwelling place. Purpose every day to live in the secret place of the Most High.

Some people continuously speak and expect calamity, "Calamity is going to come." A minister once called me concerned for our ministry. He started saying a lot of negative things. So, I said, "Don't take your can of worms and try to make it mine." Really, he was just voicing his own fears. Sometimes we tend to put our fears onto other people. Don't do that. Instead, release those fears. Get rid of them.

They (His angels) shall bear you up on their hands, lest you dash your foot against a stone.

You shall tread upon the lion and adder; the young lion and the serpent shall you trample underfoot.

Because he has set his love upon Me, therefore will I deliver him; I will set him on high, because he knows *and* understands My name [has a personal knowledge of My mercy, love, and kindness — trusts and relies on Me, knowing I will never forsake him, no, never].

He shall call upon Me, and I will answer him; I will be with him in trouble, I will deliver him and honor him.

Psalm 91:12-15

Don't talk to the devil as if he is above you. Talk to him under your feet. If you have anything to say to the devil, take your shoes and write on them and let him read it because he is under your feet.

God is telling you that He will be with you in times of trouble. God did not deliver the three Hebrew children out of the burning, fiery furnace. If He had delivered them, they would not have been put in to begin with. They still went to the furnace, but He delivered them from the fire *in* the furnace. He did not deliver Daniel from the lion's den, but from the lions *in* the den.

You never know when you will need God's protection. His angels are there to take care of you. As His child, you can be confident that He will be diligent to provide for you and to look after you. If He is concerned about your protection, don't you think He is concerned about providing for you also?

Supernatural Provision

God loves you and cares for you. The devil is the one who comes by deception and robs you of your rights and privileges. In the secret place, under that shadow of the Almighty, there is divine healing. Under the shadow of the Almighty there is supernatural provision. As you live and dwell daily in His presence, you shall not lack. The Lord spoke this to me and I want to share what He told me. He said, "If you will live daily in My presence, you will never lack. If you will live daily in My presence, and do what I want you to do, you will never lack. Lack will be far from you and your house."

If you desire to see God's blessings unfold in your life, commit to live in His presence. Pray this prayer. "Lord, I choose to obey Your Word. As I dwell and walk in Your presence, I shall not lack. Poverty, be far from me and my household in Jesus' name. I will walk in Your blessings, Lord. I will rise above all that Hell has to offer and accept Heaven's best here on earth. Everything I set my hand to will prosper because I make You my dwelling place. You are my refuge and my fortress. Thank You, Lord, for Your provision. I accept it by faith, fully expecting a turnaround in every area of my life for wherever Your presence is, there is no lack. In Jesus' name I pray. Amen.

Other books by Rodney Howard-Browne

Flowing in the Holy Ghost
The Touch of God
Manifesting the Holy Ghost
The Reality of the Person of the Holy Spirit
Fresh Oil From Heaven
The Anointing
The Coming Revival
Thoughts On Stewardship, Volume One
Walking in the Perfect Will of God
What it Means To Be Born Again

To contact the author, write:

Rodney M. Howard-Browne
P.O. Box 292888
Tampa, Florida 33687